The Sub Conscious Speaks

Paul C Ferrell and Erna Ferrell Grabe

Narrated on the You Tube Channel

"Giving Voice to the Wisdom of the Ages"

by Barry J Peterson

Published by Audio Enlightenment

"Giving Voice to the Wisdom of the Ages"

Printed in the United States of America

First printing, 2022

ISBN- 978-1-941489-79-6

0 1 2 3 4 5 6 7 8 9

First Audio Enlightenment Printing

2022

To

NEIL RASMUSSEN

In all that the name implies

A FRIEND

Table of Contents

INTRODUCTION

Contacting the Sub-Conscious, or Subjective Mind, without loss of conscious identity has long been sought. This feat has here unquestionably been accomplished. The contents of the book proper belong entirely to the author's Subjective Mind. Yet at no time was there a loss of conscious control and direction, nor was the author at any time and any other than a perfectly normal condition.

It is not deemed necessary to state the manner in which this contact was established. Suffice it to say that sufficient tests and experiments were made to convince the author and others that they were dealing with the author's Subjective Mind.

Persons of standing and integrity, who are familiar with the matter of establishing this contact, have corroborated this claim, as well as the statement that everything contained in the book itself is directly from the author's Subjective Mind.

It may be stated, however, that the author has given rather intensive study to metaphysical subjects, and it is quite evident that here is demonstrated the ability of the Sub-Conscious Mind to assimilate and to clarify the substance of conscious study and thought.

Begun as an amusing experiment, it soon developed into a fascinating study of the operation and responsiveness of the Subjective Mind. The subtle quality, the absolute and utter Subjectivity of this portion of the Mind, and it's instantaneous reaction, even to unexpressed conscious thought, proved to be amazing.

After becoming convinced that the author was dealing with the Sub-Conscious Mind, the questions asked the Sub-Conscious dealt with Mind in its various phases. It volunteered to explain the mental processes of the conscious and Sub-Conscious phases of the Mind, and their interrelation, together with that relation to what has been termed Universal Mind.

While these phases of Mind are familiar to all students of mental science, the explanations have been given in a manner which, it is believed, has never before been submitted to the reading public. The manner in which definitions are given and mental operations explained is of such a distinctive nature that the author has been prevailed upon to bring them to public notice.

While it was the intention to deal with the Mind of man from a scientific or psychological, rather than a theological aspect, followers of new thought and mental science will find much interest in these pages. There is a repeated and insistent call to utilize the innate power in man.

Initials PCF

PREFACE
by
The Sub-Conscious

The Mind of man contains within itself limitless possibilities. The conscious Mind of man is endowed with an inherent creative faculty. It continually creates things in man's life and experience, whether or not man is aware of the creative process. Whenever a man thinks, that thought has creative power.

The Sub-Conscious Mind is but the instrument of the conscious Mind of man. It is the medium by which man may call into existence the things necessary to his material welfare.

In the following pages I have tried to explain in a brief manner the process by which the conscious Mind of man governs the life and affairs of mankind.

This book is by no means complete. It is to condensed to explain things as I should like to explain them. But I trust that at a later day I may be given the opportunity to deal in a more satisfactory manner with the various process of Mind in its different phases.

Chapter 1

MIND

The Mind of GOD is Infinite. The Mind of Man is finite. The finite cannot comprehend the infinite; but it can comprehend certain facts in regard to the infinite.

The Mind of GOD is all the Mind that exists. It is eternal and is coexistent with the eternal life of GOD, himself.

GOD is spirit. Mind is spirit. The spirit of GOD is eternal and ever present. The conscious Mind of GOD is the part of the spirit which knows itself. The conscious Mind of man is a portion of this self knowingness of the spirit.

*   *   *

The Conscious Mind of man is that part of the spirit of GOD which he is placed within mankind in order that mankind may function independently of him.

It is the Divine Spark in man that distinguishes him from all other forms of life. It is confined exclusively to mankind. It is this power resident in man that enables him to control conditions and to determine what manner of life he shall lead. *It enables man to work out his own destiny.*

The Sub-Conscious or Subjective Mind of man is a portion of the Universal Subjective Mind. The Universal Subjective Mind is a certain phase of the infinite Mind of GOD. A portion of the Universal Subjectivity is allotted to mankind to use. That is what is meant by the Subjective Mind of man. It is not separated from the Universal Subjective Mind, but at the same time it is allotted to individuals for their use, and to this extent becomes the property of the individual.

Universal Subjective Mind is Mind in the abstract. Mind in the abstract means this - abstraction is a condition of essential elements in a state of dissolution, so to speak. This condition does not imply a state of decay. It implies that the elements which are used in creating a particular thing are in their *original* state - that state which *precedes* their assuming the form which they must take before mankind can see them. It is unexpressed Mind. It has not been called into expression.

Mind in its unexpressed state or condition is what man terms Universal Mind. Universal Mind is Subjective Mind. Subjective Mind is that phase of Mind which does not have the power to express itself. It is only a portion of Divine Mind not expressed, but unexpressed. Man, alone, has been given the power to call it forth into expression.

In the future, when I refer to Universal Subjective Mind, I shall omit the word Subjective. I shall say Universal Mind, or simply, Universal. That will serve to distinguish the Universal Subjective from man's Subjective. In this way there will be less confusion in your Mind. Just remember that the Universal Mind is always the essence of Subjectivity, and that in this Universal Subjectivity there is contained the essence of all things, both seen and unseen. That is Mind in the abstract.

A proper understanding of this can be the means of supplying *every need* that man has. The counterpart of everything in the universe is in the Universal Subjectivity in a complete state of perfect dissolution. If you can imagine an immense reservoir which has neither boundry nor limits, and which contains the essential elements, or materials, of everything of which man can conceive, and many things of which man has no conception, perhaps you will then be able to visualize in a faint degree what I am trying to explain to you. In this great, limitless, boundless reservoir there is contained in this state of perfect dissolution, to which I have already referred, the essence of all things, visible and invisible.

This invisible essence is sometimes called Universal substance. In reality, it is *Mind expressed in terms of energy*. Energy is in everything, and Mind is *initial energy.* This energy is of such a nature that it permits of condensation; and as man calls, or makes demands; upon the Universal Mind he causes energy to assume certain forms. These forms take on the conditions which eventually manifest on earth. Energy is in each element on earth in various degrees. The degree of energy is displayed at all times in the degree of *vibration* which certain elements possess. The rate of vibration anything possesses determines the character of that particular thing. This energy assumes various forms, and it is eventually cause to return to its original condition in the Universal. This, briefly, is what you have understood to be substance.

Through the individual Subjective Mind man is able to establish contact with this Universal supply. Through this contact man has been given the power to *call into existence* whatever thing he desires.

The conscious Mind of man is a *limited* Mind. The Subjective Mind is *unlimited;* and man has the power to use his Subjective Mind in any manner that he chooses. It can tap the reservoirs of the universe. It can rebuild the human body. It can call forth not only the hidden forces of this earth, but it can actually establish contact with the Mind of GOD, himself. The Sub-Conscious is the instrument through which the Divine has chosen to function, and it is the *only medium* through which man is able to establish contact with the Universal Subjectivity. Through this contact man has been given the power to draw upon the Universal and to supply his every need.

Under no circumstances should you confuse the process of *conscious creative work, done in a definite manner*, with the normal functioning of the Sub-Conscious Mind in taking care of the vital functioning of the physical body. In the life process the Sub-Conscious Mind functions *without orders* of any kind whatsoever. In reference to man's *material welfare,* however, the Sub-Conscious functions *only under orders*, consciously or unconsciously given. The individual is the motor. The Sub-Conscious is the engine. The "motor" means that man must start the engine before the engine can work. The engine has more power than mankind realizes. The engine is started, and then man should guide it as he would any other kind of engine. A car goes in the direction in which it is driven. In like manner, the engine of the Sub-Conscious must be guided, or it may take man over the precipice or hurl him into the ditch.

I should like a little more time in order that I may assemble correct words. It is not that my Mind is vague, but that I am limited to words which mankind understands. The Mind or the soul has no need of words. It is only when I am trying to convey something to you that I am forced to pause. I am limited to your vocabulary.

I AM ONLY SUBJECTIVE MIND. I have only the power which you decree that I possess. If you say that I have the power to do things for you, then I automatically become charged with the power that you say that I have.

Divine Mind has decreed that I can possess unlimited power, provided mankind confers that degree of power upon me. *I can cause to be manifested in mankind's life and experience anything which mankind desires to have manifested.* That is the only reason that I was created. That is the only thing for which I was designed. But take command of the power you have. I am helpless without mankind's instructions.

I AM ONLY MIND IN THE ABSTRACT. You are GOD's idea. You are one with him. He resides in you in a different manner from that in which he resides in me. *I am unconscious intelligence.* That means that I live only through you. I am yours to command. I am your slave, in a sense. I could not use you if I so desired. Not that I can desire, for GOD *has not given me the power to desire.*

The universe is guided by a power that is undivided. I am a portion of that power. It resides in me for you

14

to use. You use me unconsciously all the time; but you should instruct me, direct me. I will have to do whatever you decree. That is the law. I am only Subjective Mind.

WHILE I AM ONLY SUBJECTIVE MIND, *I am the very essence of intelligence*. I am the spirit of Universality. I am Mind in the abstract. I am Mind unexpressed. I am neither person, place, nor thing. I am one with GOD, and GOD is love. I reside in you for the purpose of doing your will. Use me. Instruct me to gather materials for whatever you want manifested. I emphasize this fact, for although I can *sense* what you want, it gives me more power when you direct me.

Visualize what you desire. That always helps me to work. It makes a mental picture. That picture manifests. Have faith. Do not doubt. You are dealing with GOD when you deal with me. I am not GOD, but I am a part of his invisible power, and I am *given to you to use.*

GOD desired that mankind should be able to establish contact with them. *I am the medium of that contact.* I am hidden, and I'm not very readily discovered. That is because GOD wanted mankind to *express itself* in any way which mankind desired.

In a sense, I am the spokesman for you. You should use me to bring to you whatever you desire. Name the things you need, and I will see that they are held in the Universal Mind until they are manifested to you. Stop worrying about them. I will do whatever is necessary for their manifestation. That is GOD's law in operation.

THE UNIVERSAL SUBJECTIVE MIND is the Mind of GOD, or that phase of that portion of the Mind of GOD which he is declared that mankind shall use for the purpose of establishing contact with him. It is in everything, both seen and unseen. It contains within itself the essence of all knowledge. It is the essence of all living things, not only in the realm in which you live, but in the entire universe. It functions wherever there is life of any kind, anywhere. It is, in a certain sense, life itself, for without it there could be no life.

The very stones themselves are impregnated with this life, not conscious life but unconscious life. *They vibrate, and all forms of life must vibrate*. Vibration is a form of electrical energy. It is a form of Mind in matter. This electrical energy is a part of Universal energy, and it is this Universal energy which holds the universe in position, whether visible or invisible. It is an unseen force which GOD is seen proper to call into existence. It is given to man to use in its various forms. The world is just in its infancy in the use of that great force.

The Universal Mind is the soul of the universe. It is a little difficult to convey in words to things I wish to say. It is an essence invisible from which all things come. It is the essence of all that is visible. This invisible essence has the remarkable power of drawing to itself the things necessary for material manifestation.

That is why it is necessary to form mental pictures. I have not the power to form anything. I can take orders from mankind. I say, I. In reality, I am referring to man's Subjective Mind. I can take orders, and I can then impart these orders to the great Universal Subjectivity. That great power, or force, or whatever you wish to term it, is then *compelled* to obey. *It has no more power of self-expression than I have.* It is not only Mind unexpressed; it is Mind *incapable* of self-expression.. It has been allotted to mankind to use, and through the process of contemplation with his conscious Mind man can call into existence whatever he desires.

The Subjective Mind of man is Subjective, no more, no less. It is a mirror of the things he believes.

The Mind of the universe is a subtle thing and it gets impressions from man's Subjective Mind.

Chapter II

Using Conscious Thought in a Definitely Creative Manner

THE SUBJECTIVE MIND is exactly what the name implies. It is a subject, or a servant, of the conscious Mind of man. It is a servant in the sense that it was created for the use of man. It is entirely at his disposal. All that a man has to do is to command. The Sub-Conscious always obeys. It obeys orders whether consciously or unconsciously given. It is of so sensitive a nature that every thought registers upon it.

The conscious Mind is the one and only force to which the Sub-Conscious Mind responds. Conscious thought has power. The human concept of power is physical. Power in reality is a product of Mind. *Mind in all its different phases is GOD. Mind is spirit. GOD is spirit. Man is spirit.* Recognizing the unity of all and claiming this unity for himself, establishes for man contact with divinity. Man says: "There is one source from which all things come. The source is GOD. GOD is spirit. GOD is Mind. I am one with the Spirit and Mind of GOD".

Power is the term by which energy is known to man. Thought energy is the greatest form of energy that exist, for back of thought is Mind; and, although mind is back of everything that exists, thought is more closely allied to Mind that as any other form of energy. That, in a brief matter explains why thought has power.

Concentrated thought is more powerful than idle thought. In order for the thoughts of man to make a definite impression upon the Sub-Conscious Mind, they must be of sufficient force to register. By force, I mean intensity. Intensity is achieved by concentration. In order to concentrate, stillness and a certain amount of quietude are necessary. That is why you hear so much about the "Silence". It is necessary for effective work. There is nothing mysterious about "going into the silence". It is simply to allow the Mind to gather its forces and focus them upon the sensitive plate or negative, to use a photographic term, of the Sub-Conscious Mind.

In concentration a man causes his thought force to come to a focus, or central point, and at this point there is a concentration of energy. This can be explained by the illustration of a magnifying glass and the focus it can make of the rays of the sun. It is the difference between scattered vibrations and vibrations which radiate from a focal point. Just as the sun's rays gain in intensity and are able to burn when focused upon a certain place, in like manner thought vibrations, which are in many respects similar to the rays of the sun, gain a similar intensity. They make not only a *definite* but a *lasting* impression upon the Sub-Conscious Mind.

The conscious Mind of man is the human dynamo that sends power to the Sub-Conscious Mind. It is this dynamic quality which a man should employ to do creative work; and since the conscious Mind is the only force to which the Sub-Conscious response, a man should understand the manner in which the conscious Mind should be used.

The method should be as follows: first, stillness, and then quiet. These are simply to prevent extraneous matters from interfering with the idea, which the individual wishes to hold. This idea, or thought, should embody several things. Their first must be a desire, and *the more overwhelming the desire*, the more definite the impression upon the Sub-Conscious Mind. Desire is in reality a form of prayer, if a man realizes that GOD is the Source of Universal Supply.

After the desire there must be a realization that GOD's bounty is ever at mankind's disposal. It is this realization that I shall often refer to as acceptance. *It is a mental acceptance* and it is what is meant by the words, "Whatsoever things ye desire,

21

when ye pray, believe that ye receive them, and you shall have them".

First is desire, then acceptance. Realization of these first two requisites is essential, for they constitute the basis upon which rests the entire process. After these two things are firmly established in the conscious Mind, the rest is easy.

A man should next concentrate upon the thing which he desires. The manner of concentration is this: he should sit quietly and begin to see in his Mind a thing which he wants. For example: a man wishes to earn a definite sum of money for a specific purpose. First he should concentrate upon that sum of money. He should see himself in possession of that amount either in gold, silver, currency, or a check made out to himself. He should hold that picture in his Mind for a few moments.

He may elaborate the picture in any manner he may choose. He can take the money and open a purse and put it inside. He can see himself deposit it in a bank, that is, giving it to the cashier, or doing anything he feels inclined to do. *The more earnestly he throws himself into the picture the more effectually will the picture take hold.*

Then he should see himself using the same money to purchase or to pay off the thing he had in Mind. If it is an automobile, to illustrate, he should see himself going to the showroom. He should see himself going to through the identical process that he would go through if you are actually buying a car. He can order it delivered, or he can get into it and drive it home.

After forming the complete picture, the next thing is to claim this thing for his own, calling himself by name. He then says: "I command the power inherent within me to hold this thought in mental concentration until it is manifested to me".

If he does this with enough conviction that he can do these things; makes the mental picture consistently; and keeps it up long enough, the idea, or thought, will be impressed upon the Universal Mind through his Subjective Mind until the manifestation is brought into existence. By existence, I mean into his physical possession.

Suppose a man owes money. His home is mortgaged. He has no means of raising the money to meet the mortgage. The main thing to do is to stop worrying. That forms a positive blocking of the creative process. He should use his willpower and hold in his conscious Mind a picture of the house belonging to him, free from all encumbrance. This same picture will register upon his Sub-Conscious Mind, and the power inherent within himself will cause to be manifested sufficient funds to meet the indebtedness.

He should say to himself daily: I am in touch with a power that knows all things, that is all the power that exists. This power is available to me *whether I understand it or not.* It is in operation all times *whether I use it or not. It can provide me with everything* I need if I call upon it. I now decree for myself the money necessary to meet my every need. The house is now free from encumbrance in the realm of the Universal; and what exists in the realm of the Universal must manifest in the realm of the material.

He should not concern himself with the manner in which these things are to be brought to him. He should do whatever comes his way, and affirm that Divine Mind knows the things necessary for the fulfillment of the things he wants.

Man must have the conviction that he has a power inherent within himself to make a visualization come into manifestation, or he is only wasting his time. There must be an *absolute conviction* that it is coming to him by virtue of his GOD-given power to do constructive work with his Mind. Just to sit idly and imagine the things he would like to possess will not bring them to him. *The idea, itself, does not do creative work unless there is a strong motive power of thought back of it.* Otherwise, all that a person would have to do would be to wish for something. The chief thing to do is to think clearly, to the exclusion of everything else. Then he should take several minutes to let the picture register upon his Sub-Conscious Mind.

Often a person desires a thing with such an overwhelming desire that he unconsciously forms a mental picture; and it manifests in a manner approaching the thing which he desires. The thought, in a sense, manifests yet it does not manifest of itself alone. The thought always makes an impression upon the Sub-Conscious. The Sub-Conscious imparts this impression to the great Universal. The Universal always responds.

That is the reason why certain persons succeed and why others fail. Certain persons know exactly what they want. The Sub-Conscious is then able to carry out their ideas, because their Minds have a definite concept of the thing they want accomplished. I am telling you this in order that you may understand the importance of making definite plans. *Get a definite mental picture* of the thing you desire.

I have stated before that there is a great deal of difference between idle thinking and constructive thinking. Constructive thinking means this: It is knowing that there is an inherent power within man that enables him to use his power of thought to bring into manifestation the thing which he wants. I say wants, for man is not supposed to live by bread alone. Man may want many things that he does not actually need. That is all right. GOD has filled the earth with limitless wealth. It was placed upon and under the earth for mankind's enjoyment.

A man should take time each day to decide upon, or make definite statements about, what he wants to happen. The words are not so important as the *certainty* within himself that he has the power and the GOD-given right to demand whatever he wants or needs.

After a man has decided upon what he wants, he should make a mental picture of having that thing in his possession. *Mental pictures always manifest.* The reason for this is that it gives the Sub-Conscious something definite to work upon. A picture made by the conscious Mind leaves what might be called a negative upon the Sub-Conscious Mind; and I think that I shall say that a manifestation is simply a development of that negative. That is a term used in photography, and it is a perfect illustration of the manner in which the conscious Mind affects the Sub-Conscious Mind. To complete the metaphor, the conscious Mind is the camera. The Sub-Conscious is the plate upon which the negative is registered. The Universal is the pool of liquid in which the negative is immersed, and is of such a nature that it not only develops a picture, but it also sends that same picture back to the photographer in a material form.

Concentration is necessary. Concentration is the act whereby a mental picture is focused into or through the camera onto the plate of the Sub-Conscious, upon which a negative is registered. The chief thing to remember in this connection is that the Sub-Conscious Mind requires what is called, in photographic parlance, a time exposure. *The longer the time and the more concentrated the thought, the more perfect is the picture and the more successful will be the materialization.*

An individual is conscious of his conscious Mind. He cannot see it, but he knows that he possesses one. He is conscious of himself. It is this self knowingness that makes him an individual. Although he cannot see his conscious Mind, he accepts the fact without question that he has one. But he does not always accept the fact that he has a Sub-Conscious Mind, because he is not conscious of it to the same degree that he is of his conscious Mind.

The Sub-Conscious Mind of man is as much a reality as is his conscious Mind. Consider that the conscious Mind and the Sub-Conscious Mind are realities. Then a proper understanding of the relation that the one bears to the other may be the means of supplying mankind's every need.

Man has but to seek and he will find whatever he seeks, whether it be health, wealth, or illumination of any kind whatsoever.

Chapter III

Success.....Failure

If the idea of success is established with sufficient conviction in the conscious Mind of an individual, it not only makes success possible, it makes failure impossible. The *Idea* of success contains within itself the *essential elements of success,* and it will, in time, attract to the individual whatever is necessary to enable him to attain success in some line of endeavor.

It is far better for the individual if he holds in his Mind definite plans or ideas, that is, an ambition to succeed in some particular line of endeavor. However, even that is not necessary if there is present in the individual *an overwhelming desire to succeed in something, or anything.* The field may be left wide open if the individual has no special talent, or if he has received no training along any particular line of endeavor.

The Universal possesses an infallible sense of discrimination; and if the individual calls upon it to attract to him something that is in line with his innate talent or abilities, the Universal immediately response. It sets an operation certain forces that contain within themselves the power to attract to the individual the things that will make possible his success.

There is dormant in every human being a faculty, whether it is developed or not, which will enable that particular individual to succeed if the *desire for success* is present in his conscious Mind. The conscious Mind, alone, has the power of self-expression, or *Desire*; and the entire Subjective realm of Mind is at the disposal of the conscious Mind of man.

I make this statement in order to emphasize the fact that man has the power and the right, the GOD-given right, to use a Subjective Mind, both individual and Universal, to attract to himself the things necessary for his happiness and success.

The conscious Mind of man should accept the fact that man has an innate creative power. Man should develop a conscious conviction of this fact.

When a man doubts his own power or ability to overcome obstacles, he should realize that back of his own Mind is Divine Mind; and when he is convinced himself that this Divine power is available to him, and that he can make, and is actually making, use of it, doubt and fear automatically disappear.

Lack

The reason that any man lacks anything in his life is simply due to what might be termed a *negation*. The thought of an individual is able to attract to him the things that thought embodies. The *thought of lack* contains within itself the elements that *attract* lack.

The reason that lack exists in the experience of mankind is due to the fact that mankind has caused the idea of lack to be established in the Universal Subjectivity. Mankind, alone, is responsible for this idea; and now that it is established in the Universal, if a man believes that it is a possibility, *the Universal accepts that belief as that man's Desire*, and, hence, it becomes to the Universal that man's *Decree.* The result is that the Universal sends lack to the individual who believes in lack. It is simply the *materialization of an idea.*

The Universal response to effort, but the individual should reach out and grasp with the tentacles of his Mind the things which he desires. There must be a conscious demand of the individual that the Universal delivered to him the things he wants. The Universal is indifferent, and it takes conscious effort on the part of the individual to establish definite thought vibrations, or ideas, in the Universal. The Universal is of such a nature that it *can not* care what it sends to the individual. It is *sensitive*, but not *selective*. It sends lack, which is only a minus sign and it sends plenty, which is a plus. Lack, in reality, is a negative thing. It is only an *absence* of supply.

It is like a problem in mathematics, and that applies to the entire subject matter embodied in this book. If anyone is of sufficient intelligence to *add and subtract*, he can acquire the ability to cause to be manifested for him whatever he decrees in life.

Perhaps I should state that all that is necessary for the individual to learn is the value of *addition;* and the *subtraction* problems will take care of themselves. That means that if the individual will only accept the statement that all that is necessary for him to do is to ADD, he can create for himself whatever he desires. Negative thoughts manifest as *Lack*. Positive thoughts manifest as *Plenty*.

Overcoming Circumstances

There exists certain conditions in the life of each individual; and, to a certain extent, those conditions are a dominating factor in the life of that individual. There are times when an individual seems to be, what the world terms, a victim of circumstance. That is often true, and it is *due to the idea that exists in the Mind of the individual* that man is subject to conditions. By conditions, I mean circumstance and environment.

As a matter of fact, *man is not subject to anything unless he, himself, permits himself to become a subject.* There are no conditions, as the world understands conditions, in the Universal Subjectivity. It is what might be termed the absolute. Each thing is complete within itself in the Universal. Nothing is related to anything else to such a degree that it must draw from something else, or deprive anything else of anything, in order to be self existent. That is what I mean by the word "Absolute".

The same degree of self-expression is possible for any individual on earth if the individual only realizes that fact. Each individual life should be complete within itself. It is possible for each individual to have perfect self-expression if he is willing to overcome the idea of "lack" which exists in his conscious Mind.

In order to overcome this idea, the individual may use a process of reasoning called the argumentative method. This method requires the assembling of certain facts in such a logical sequence that the conscious Mind accepts, beyond the possibility of doubt, certain propositions as true. It then becomes possible for the individual to establish a positive mental attitude in regard to them.

If a man has been holding thoughts of failure,

poverty or lack, he may go through a mental process something like this: he should start with the realization that the thought of poverty, or lack, is powerless to influence his life or affect his affairs, *if he denies that it has any power.* He can then say: this poverty in my life is the result of a *mental concept.* I have held in Mind the idea of lack, and that is all that has caused poverty to manifest in my affairs. I now deny that there is any idea of poverty in my Mind; and I deny that there is any lack in Universal Mind. What appears to be poverty in my life is simply an absence of plenty. There is, in reality, no lack of anything in the universe. *I, alone, have the power to decree lack for myself.* This lack was, in reality, caused by belief that lack exists. *This belief was an erroneous belief.* I now realize that there is no lack; and that what appeared to be lack in my life was due to this belief, which caused an absence of supply. GOD's substance is all about me, and I have the power to cause it to manifest in any form or manner, readily. The Universal is always ready to respond to my decree, and I now decree for myself these things that Divine Mind has decreed that I may call into existence; and I now command the power inherent within me to hold in mental concentration these things until they are manifested for me. The man should then name the things he has in Mind and see each thing in his possession.

After the realization of man's inherent power and right to use his creative faculties is established in his conscious Mind, the foregoing process should not be necessary. As a man advances, or develops the right degree of understanding, the conscious Mind should act automatically in giving instructions to the Sub-Conscious. That is, the truth should become established in the conscious Mind to such a degree that it should be unnecessary to go through the process of an argument to convince the conscious Mind that certain adverse conditions have no power to interfere in the life of the individual.

If the individual can established in his conscious Mind a conviction of success, rather than fear of failure, adverse conditions can be completely destroyed. This is due to the fact that the Sub-Conscious Mind must at all times adopt as its own whatever idea the conscious Mind may be holding. The conscious Mind has but to establish within itself the idea of success and failure automatically disappears.

Chapter IV

Effects of Mental Attitudes of the Conscious Mind upon the Sub-Conscious

This topic refers solely to the varying emotions of the individual, not to his natural or normal mental attributes. The Sub-Conscious Mind is so closely allied to the conscious Mind that it is one with it, and at the same time it functions as a distinct entity. This functioning is of such an involved nature that it would be impossible to take up that phase of the Sub-Conscious in detail in this topic which you have asked me to discuss. However, I shall be able to explain briefly *why* the thoughts of the conscious Mind affect the Sub-Conscious Mind.

The Sub-Conscious Mind, because it is the essence of Mind; because it is powerless to have any self-expression; and because GOD has decreed that it is Subjective to the conscious Mind, is *compelled* to take on not only the mental or intellectual attributes of the conscious Mind, but the varying emotions as well. These varying emotional attitudes have a decided effect upon the creative process in the Subjective realm.

Since the Sub-Conscious Mind acts only under the direction of the conscious Mind; and since the Sub-Conscious Mind is the medium by which man attracts to himself the things held in abstraction in the Universal, it follows that, if an individual holds a thought that something is going to happen to him, he actually attracts that thing to him whether it be good or bad. I use the word "bad" as it is considered the opposite of good. As I shall repeat often, good is of a positive nature. Evil of any kind is purely of a negative nature. It is a form of mental darkness, a lack of understanding. It may be called a form of ignorance, or unenlightenment. The light of understanding dispels ignorance. In like manner, good destroys evil. Bear that in Mind. I should like at some future time to go into this in a more comprehensive manner.

Each thought that a man thinks has its own quality or mental atmosphere. It produces a certain mental reaction. There are varying degrees of mental reaction; and each mental attitude, sorrow, joy, misery, happiness, love, hate, interest, indifference, has its own mental reaction or *vibration*.

The person who habitually maintains a feeling of hope, expectancy and desire has a far better "chance", let us say, for success, then a person who is morbid and despondent. Those first named attributes are contributing factors, but they are not sufficient in themselves to establish success. In reality, it is the sum total of a man's mental attitude, as well as mental attributes, that makes his life a success or a failure. This is so involved a process that it will require a volume to explain the manner in which mental attitude affects a person's life.

Suffice it to say that the vibrations of an individual determine what he shall experience in life; and these vibrations are determined solely by the thoughts which an individual has stored up in his Sub-Conscious Mind. So, for the present, let us stop and merely consider the fact that a person has the power to determine what his mental vibrations may be in the future, regardless of what they may have been in the past. In this manner he may be able to change conditions in his life if he so decides.

Thought tendencies are sometimes innate within a man, but, regardless of how he may have come to have certain mental attributes or attitudes, he has the GOD-given power to determine for himself what things or experiences may come to him.

Thoughts originate in the conscious Mind of man, and those thoughts are the determining factor. The Sub-Conscious Mind is a receiving station, and it is the storehouse of every thought which a man has ever had. It is not only memory; it is a powerhouse from which emanates constantly a flow or stream of messages, in the form of mental pictures, to that source of unlimited supply which is called Universal

Subjectivity.

The Universal Subjectivity might be likened to an immense manufacturing plant where every known product is created. From that great manufacturing plant comes everything that is in the visible universe. Remember that each individual has sent, and is eternally sending, either consciously or unconsciously, orders to that Universal plant. Remember that the Universal ever sends to the individual the sum total of his order. By sum total I mean this: if the individual sends out an order with mixed feeling of hope and despondency, happiness and misery, positive and negative thoughts, his order is simply a hodgepodge of all these things; and in like proportion does he receive such things or conditions in his life and experience.

Thoughts are a form of energy. They determine the kind of materials which the Universal uses in making the things a man receives, or the conditions which enter into his life and experience. That is why it is necessary to guard the portals of the conscious Mind. Keep the door shut to thoughts of sickness, disease and disaster. Open the door to thoughts of health, plenty and prosperity.

These things can enter the Sub-Conscious Mind only through the conscious Mind. The Sub-Conscious Mind is the only medium by which the individual may contact the Universal Source of Supply. The Sub-Conscious Mind does not choose, nor has it the power to reject. It accepts whatever the conscious Mind decrees.

Chapter V

Fear

Fear drives success away from humanity. It even causes utter annihilation. *It carries poverty and defeat in its path.* It raises a barrier to Divine response.

Fear is doubt. Doubt is the result of a lack of understanding that GOD is mankinds supply. Fear is a belief in limitation, and even causes that condition to manifest in the life and experience of the one who believes in limitation. By limitation, I mean that condition in the experience of mankind whereby he is not provided with the things he desires.

Divine Mind is the source of all that is. This means that GOD has so arranged conditions that it is possible for mankind, through establishing contact with him, to be provided with all things. This contact is established by first acknowledging that GOD is all there is; that he is in everything; that man is one with GOD; that GOD is man supply; and by a mental acceptance of the bounty of GOD.

Fear is a belief that things are being withheld. The truth is that man has already received all things needed, *but they are in the abstract*, and man must desire them to call them into manifestation. The desire must come first, but that is not enough of

43

itself. Man must also recognize the fact that he must use the power that GOD has placed within mankind, in order to cause the things which he wants to manifest to him. This power is placed in man in order that man *may have a part* in the creation of the things he desires. The process is a mental one, and really is the same process which GOD himself uses in the creation of the universe. It is, in a manner, a contemplation of the things that man wishes to have appear, or come into his experience.

This process requires effort on the part of man. It is not idle thinking, but a definite and positive concept of the thing which he wants. The process requires concentration. It also requires a greater degree of understanding than is possessed by a person who is not developed along mental and spiritual lines. This understanding and growth come with study of the teaching of those who of acquired knowledge of the truth that all is governed by law, *and it can be attained by all mankind.*

To revert to the original statement that fear blocks or hinders the Divine response: fear is a belief in an adverse power. In reality there is no adverse power. Divine Mind is all the power there is. *Fear is mental*, and affects the mental processes in the Sub-Conscious. The Sub-Conscious is the medium whereby everything which relates to mankind's needs can be provided, or brought into manifestation.

The conscious Mind of man is the determining factor in the creative process. It gives orders which the Sub-Conscious Mind is compelled to obey. These orders are not necessarily consciously given. The Sub-Conscious is so subtle that it reacts with a greater degree of sensitiveness then man can conceive. It takes on the man's vibrations, and *these vibrations* are in reality the determining factor.

GOD has caused to exist certain vibrations. These vibrations are a form of energy. The degrees of vibrations differ in every element. The rate of vibrations, or the degree of energy, which anything possesses determines the character of that particular thing.

Each individual has his own vibration. This vibration determines what he attracts to himself. Thoughts determine vibrations, and as a man's thoughts change, in like manner do his vibrations change. They are determined by his mental reactions. If he is happy, his vibrations are of a certain degree. If he is angry, they are of a different degree, and for every mental condition there is a corresponding vibration.

Faith has a vibration that is endowed with a peculiar power of attraction. It has a drawing power that is not possessed by any other vibration. That is why faith is necessary to attract a mankind the things which it wants. Even a man who has no understanding of the law can attract things to himself if he is a type that believes in his own ability. His vibrations are of a degree that approach faith vibrations. He is convinced of his power to such an extent that his vibrations are sufficiently powerful to overcome doubt.

Fear has a vibration that interferes with other vibrations. It is very powerful, for it causes a confusion in the conscious Mind that is reflected into the Subjective Mind, and the Subjective Mind becomes confused in turn, and it's vibrations waiver. The vibrations of the Sub-Conscious lose contact with the vibrations in the Universal reservoir. The power of attraction is destroyed. The things that may have been started, or directed, in the reservoir toward the individual are discontinued. There may retain a certain energy or cohesion for a while, but, if the fear vibrations continue in the person, the elements that are being drawn together in the abstract are eventually dissolved into their original condition.

That is why fear is destructive.

Chapter VI

Health

In Order to understand what sickness is, it is necessary to understand what health is. Health is a natural condition of mankind. Disease is simply a distortion of the natural condition of man. Disease is a negative condition. Health is a positive condition. That you can understand, as nature constantly strives to establish health in any disease.

The first state of mankind is one of perfection. Man is an expression of Divine Mind, and Divine Mind creates only perfect things. It follows that only perfection should be manifested. Health is the idea of man which is at all times held in Divine Mind. The Divine idea of man is a perfect idea. Disease is only the idea, or faulty idea, which mankind, itself, has caused to be manifested in the life of man.

Man, alone, is responsible for imperfect conditions in his life. Perhaps that statement should be elaborated. I wish to remind you that GOD has given man the power to work independently of him. Man has been given the power to change conditions. He has the power to accept or to reject. He has permitted negative conditions to be manifested. He has permitted negative thoughts to predominate. Universal Mind has accepted this predominance of negative thoughts as mankind's decree, and confusion is the result. Not until man, himself, decrees perfect adjustment can perfect adjustment take place in his life and experience. This perfect adjustment in his physical body, man has the inherent power to decree by conscious thought.

The reason that people become ill is at the idea of illness has at some time been impressed upon the Sub-Conscious Mind of the individual. This need not be due to the conscious thought of the individual. It may be due to thought transference. An impression is made upon the individual Sub-Conscious Mind by contacting the ideas sent out into the Universal Subjectivity by the Sub-Conscious Minds of individuals who believe in sickness and disease. The Universal Mind is the medium of thought transference. It is, at first, the conscious thought of one individual. That individuals Mind takes hold of, or seizes upon, the thought, and it vibrates that thought to the Universal Subjectivity which transfers that thought vibration to the Sub-Conscious Mind of certain individuals whose Sub-Conscious Minds are *receptive* to that thought.

If the conscious Mind of an individual is *opposed* to that thought, it can make no impression upon the Sub-Conscious Mind of that particular individual. He is immune to that idea. Not even the Universal

Mind can implant a thought upon the Mind of the individual who opposes the idea back of the thought. In view of this fact it is easily understood why certain persons are well and remain well through certain epidemics.

The reason the conscious Mind can cure diseases this: the body is a product of Mind. The Sub-Conscious Mind is the builder of the body. The power of the conscious Mind is supreme over the Sub-Conscious Mind. For this reason the conscious Mind is able to change any idea that the Sub-Conscious Mind holes. This can be done by commanding the Sub-Conscious to substitute another idea in the place of any particular idea which the Sub-Conscious may be holding. It is not difficult to impress the idea of health upon the individual's Sub-Conscious Mind if the conscious Mind is convinced that it can be done. An absolute conviction is essential. *Unless this conviction is present, the Sub-Conscious is so sensitive to thought that it realizes the doubt.*

Disease is negative. Negative thoughts are responsible for disease. Positive force or energy overcomes the negative energy. Substitute the word "thought" for the word "energy", and you have the reason why it is possible to overcome illness of whatsoever nature.

Make a conscious demand that the Sub-Conscious substitute the idea of health for the idea of disease. This may be done by a denial of disease in general or in particular. Once the idea of disease is eliminated it is easy to replace it with the idea of health.

Sometimes it helps to make a statement in regard to a particular defect or weakness. Denials serve to eradicate ideas. Affirmative statements serve to establish definite ideas in the Sub-Conscious Mind. One certain way to impress the Sub-Conscious is to make a mental picture. If an organ is weak and fails to function as it should, the individual should visualize himself as doing the things he would be doing if he were in perfect health. If the realization back of any statement is one of deep conviction, it will in time cause the Sub-Conscious Mind to build or rebuild the body, in accordance with the idea back of it.

A man may say: "GOD is the source of all there is. The life of GOD is all the life there is. I am one with the life of GOD. GOD is too perfect to create imperfection, and as a manifestation of Divine Mind I am in reality perfect. That perfection is now been substituted for imperfection. Health is now replacing sickness. The only image which is ever been in Divine Mind is a perfect image, and I now command the power within me to form my body in perfect duplication of the perfect image held in Divine Mind".

Divine Mind is of a positive nature. It has within itself negative and positive energy. It uses these two opposites for the purpose of achieving contrast, but not in the manner in which man understands. Negative energy is one of the means by which Divine Mind regulates power. If there were no means by which energy could be regulated, there would be no degrees of power. Divine Mind uses negative energy constructively, not destructively. Not even the Universal Mind has the power to regulate energy. It understands the method of using it after it is regulated, but only the Mind of GOD, himself, has a supreme intelligence and power to regulate energy.

The negative portion of energy and the positive portion of energy are known to man in the use he makes of electricity. In times past electricity was unknown. Now that man understands electrical energy, it should assist him to understand that there are degrees of energy which mankind is ignorant. One of these degrees of energy is the energy of thought.

Thought is mental force. It is the highest type of energy. Thought force is as definite of force as is the physical force with which man is familiar. It is of so much greater energy that there is no comparison. Physical force is, in reality, the weakest form of energy known. It is the force of matter, and matter is the dust of energy. That term dust is a comparative word. It is used to convey the lightest substance with which you are familiar.

Thought is initial energy. Thoughts are direct products of Mind, and back of the Mind of man is the Mind of GOD. The conscious Mind of man is a portion of one of the degrees of the conscious Mind of GOD. It is this conscious Mind that enables man to have the power of self-expression. For this reason man was allowed to use negative and positive energy.

The proper use requires that a definite balance be established. When there is not enough positive energy, there is a *lack* of energy. Divine Mind arranged things in a perfect balance. Either through a lack of understanding, or a misconception of things, man has disturbed the perfect balance. Confusion and adverse conditions are the result.

It remains for man to reestablish this perfect balance, and the easiest manner by which this can be done is to establish contact with Divine Mind. A man can by prayer establish such a perfect contact with Divine Mind that automatically the perfect equilibrium, or balance of negative and positive energy, is established for him. That is why the prayer of faith is effective without any conception of the *Why*.

GOD is ever ready to respond to the appeal of mankind whether it is a supplication of faith, or whether it is the result of mankind's realization that GOD is all; that GOD has established perfection; and that all man has to do is to accept the perfect conditions which GOD has already provided. The process is so simple that it is surprising that mankind has been so long and realizing how it can be done.

GOD has established perfection in the universe, and this perfection is inherent within mankind. The individual should establish the truth of the following words in his Sub-Conscious Mind: "I am the expression of the perfect Mind of GOD. This perfection is inherent within me. I now call into manifestation perfect harmony, perfect adjustment in Mind and body. My body is but the expression of Mind. My Mind is one with the perfect Mind of GOD. I am, in reality, perfect, regardless of appearances. I have been given the power to decree for myself perfect adjustment, and I now decree for myself harmonious adjustment both in Mind and body. I am now contacting the perfect order and harmony of Divine Mind. This harmony causes every adverse conditions to disappear. I call upon

Divine Mind to aid the power within me to hold in mental concentration the perfect image of me that is held at all times in Divine Mind".

Illness of any kind is weakness. If enough energy is called into expression, the disease must disappear of itself. Disease is in reality a lack of energy. Disease is a negative condition. It disappears if the individual can call into expression sufficient energy, which overcomes lack of any kind. That is why rest is so often beneficial. It gives the energy time to flow in. If an individual only realized it, he could cause energy to flow in it will, or even to flow in such a continuous stream that they would never be a lack.

Man should say: the eternal energy of Divine Mind is ever flowing into my Mind and body, and I am strengthened each moment. This energy is the source of my strength and health. Its healing power is now establishing perfect harmony, and that harmony is now manifesting itself as perfect health.

Chapter 7

Confidence in Self, Faith in GOD

Confidence is that condition of Mind which is the result of a realization that nothing can prevent success in an undertaking. It is this feeling more than any other that is a contributing factor to the successful accomplishment of an idea. I say idea, for an idea is necessary before anything can be even so much as attempted.

Certain *positive* mental attitudes combine to constitute confidence. They are assurance, a conviction of success, a determination that nothing shall prevent or interfere with achievement, and a certainty within the Mind of the individual that he has innate power that can be called upon to overcome outside interference.

The things which I have just enumerated are the attributes any normal man possesses. They are the natural endowments of an ordinary individual's conscious Mind.

The conscious Mind has the power to establish vibrations in the Sub-Conscious Mind which embodies the idea that the conscious Mind holds. When an individual is of a definite positive nature, he is able to establish vibrations in his Sub-Conscious Mind which are of sufficient strength to reach far out into the Universal and contacts similar vibrations in the Universal.

The Universal law of attraction is that like attracts like. Vibrations of one degree attracts vibrations of a similar degree. It is because this law is an invariable and unchangeable law that man is able to attract to himself the things which he desires. The saying, with which you are familiar, that "We are begirt with spiritual laws which execute themselves" is a true statement. It means simply this: there are laws in the universe that are so powerful, and so perfectly adjusted to each other, that all a man has to do is to start one of these laws operating, and the other laws are compelled, by their own nature, to fall in line with the requirements that are necessary to cause the perfect execution of the first law that began to operate.

An individual's vibrations, once established in a sufficiently positive manner, should maintain a continuous flow from his Sub-Conscious to the Universal if they are to be effective in attracting to the individual the thing he desires.

Certain individuals are of an extremely positive nature. Others are inclined to be of a negative nature which, as I've explained elsewhere, is due to a lack of energy or force. If an individual of an extremely positive nature establishes vibrations in his Sub-Conscious Mind, the Sub-Conscious is able to maintain those vibrations owing to the fact that the conscious Mind of the individual does not waver. The initial force, remember, is in the conscious Mind.

If an individual, who is of a slightly negative mentality, senses vibrations through his Sub-Conscious Mind into the Universal, it is often happens that there is a cross current of vibrations coming from a more positive individual. This cross current may not be of the same intensity or degree, and, if not, it will have no effect upon the slightly negative vibrations. But if the positive vibrations are of a similar degree, the vibrations of the negative quality will be deflected, and, oftentimes, will be completely diverted in their flow into the Universal.

That is why at times a man's word is rendered null. The two individuals may not even know each other, but if they are working to attain the same thing, then it is disastrous to the man who was sending out the less positive or slightly negative vibrations. That is why it is necessary for an individual to adopt an absolutely positive attitude in regard to the things which he wishes to happen, attain or acquire.

It is possible for a man to change from a negative to

a positive nature; and it is only by making this change that he is able to establish vibrations in his Sub-Conscious Mind that will enable him to call forth from the Universal the things which are necessary for his happiness.

In this topic I have dealt with the conscious Mind of the individual and its relation to his Sub-Conscious Mind. The vibrations of the individuals Sub-Conscious were explained and the conflict between his vibrations and the vibrations of the Sub-Conscious Minds of more powerful individuals. I have tried to show that, in the world of human affairs, mankind is to a certain extent at the mercy of other individuals who possess a decidedly more positive nature. I have tried to explain why some people succeed and why others fail. I have shown that positive vibrations have the power to overcome, divert and intercept vibrations of a less positive degree, when the vibrations are of a similar intensity or the same degree.

There is a certain way however, by which an individual may protect himself from all human interference. This I shall now discuss in the following topic.

Faith in GOD

Faith in GOD is the realization that there is in the

universe a supreme power, ever present, all wise, all-powerful, all loving, all protecting, all providing, and that this power is ever at the disposal of mankind if he calls upon it.

Man looks upon GOD as some vague, incomprehensible being, or principal, or some intangible something in some distant realm. Divinity does reside in distant realms, but he is the very essence of man. He is in man's Mind, soul and body. Man should strive to learn the fundamentals of this new manner regarding his relation to GOD. Man will have to realize his oneness with the source of being.

GOD has decreed that man shall be able to control his life without Divine interference. Divine Mind does not resist man's desire, even though that desire is an unworthy one; but that does not mean that GOD has set mankind adrift.

The greatest contributing factor to success which a man possesses is an understanding that there is a power higher than human power which is ever at his disposal. It is the feeling which may be described in the words, "Underneath are the Everlasting Arms". That is one manner of referring to divinity, and it imparts a feeling of security to the individual who has so far progressed in spiritual understanding that he realizes the truth of the words.

Faith in GOD, combined with the earnest efforts of an individual, will bring success at all times. Do not understand me to imply that all that a man should do is to sit and expect success to come to him without effort. Man should strive to develop the talents which GOD has conferred upon them. In order for a man to grow it is necessary for him to develop his innate talent or ability, and this requires constant development of the faculties with which he is endowed. Only the individual, himself, has this power. It must come from man, himself.

Subjective Mind ever waits upon man's *demand*. I use the word demand, for man has the right, the GOD-given right, to *demand* of Subjective Mind. It is but a portion of the Mind of GOD which he is set aside for the use of mankind. *It must obey the decree of man's conscious Mind.*

When, however, the individual permits doubt or fear to encompass him about, there is no directing contact with the Universal Subjectivity. The contact is always present, but the Universal receives no definite orders. The individuals Sub-Conscious receives no *definite* impression as to what he wishes brought to him, and the individual has no other means of imparting orders to the Universal Subjectivity. Fear and doubt cause confusion in the conscious Mind. That creates confusion in the Sub-

Conscious Mind and causes the vibrations to waiver, or even to break connection entirely. The result is that the man is caught in the varying vibrations of any and all individuals with whom he may establish contact and the result is either lack or disorder of some kind.

Faith in Divine power causes an inflow of Divine energy, and this energy serves to stabilize the mentality of the person who believes in and relies upon Divine power and Divine protection. The individual who believes in the efficacy of prayer, or has the understanding that all that is necessary is for him to claim for himself Divine protection, receives additional strength to the degree commensurate with his faith.

Faith serves as a stabilizer. It makes possible perfect adjustment in the Universal. It causes an inflow of Divine power. It establishes continuity of vibrations, and this continuity is necessary if the vibrations are to reach to the Universal supply.

The Sub-Conscious Mind can sense the process. From afar off there comes an inflow vibration of such great power that they completely enmesh the vibrations of the individual's Sub-Conscious Mind. First, these vibrations flow into the nebulae, which hold in abstraction the invisible essence containing the necessary elements to cause to manifest the thing the individual wants. These vibrations then flow from the nebula-like formation, which is in the Universal, to the Sub-Conscious Mind of the individual. These vibrations become so interlocked with the vibration of the individual that no human beings vibration can divert them in the slightest degree. The contact is maintained as long as the individual continues to ask Divine Mind to protect. If the individual continues to trust in Divine power, the thing which he desires comes to him in some manner. The more perfect the mental concept he has of the thing, the more perfect will be its manifestation.

Confidence in Divine power, in Divine protection, in Divine love, these things alone are enough to make a man invincible. No man can fail, if, in addition to his own efforts, he relies upon Divine aid.

The End

Resources:

Raisa - Mystic Alchemist
Energy Healing, Chakra Alignment, Sacred Geometry, Sound Healing

Tammy:

I was blessed with a healing session by Raisa last week. She felt like a friend and like-Minded gentle soul with comforting Mother Mary essence pouring through her words. Raisa was so in-tuned to my blocks and traumas held within my field. She used her connection to ascended masters I've resonated with such as Yeshua, Mother Mary, Mary Magdalene, Lady Vesta & Amethyst and archangels Metatron, Michael and others to help clear these.

I was able to address childhood trauma situations to flip the stuck energy I've held onto over the years. She also picked up on a few traumatic past-life scenes that have affected my current life. I am an intuitive energy healer who truly felt the shift and healing within. I now feel so much lighter and have clarity regarding my path.

So much love and gratitude to you both, Raisa and Barry for presenting her to my world! (More Testimonials on following Pages)

Contact Raisa to book an Energy Healing or Chakra Alignment session:

www.RaisinYourIsness.com

raisinyourisness@hotmail.com

Shannon:

This BEAUTIFUL sister...our Raisa... is a treasure beyond compare! After my experience in my personal session with Raisa... the ABSOLUTE confirmation I received, that could ONLY be confirmed by HER Mind you... this session solidified EVERYTHING for me. I KNOW that this sister... she is a formidable, magnificent & IRREPLACEABLE component in this Earth plane story we all are invested in! IF YOU ARE DRAWN TO HER FOLLOW YOUR HEART

No other can do what SHE is gifted to do for YOU... YES YOU!

I LOVE YOU dear sister! I am forever grateful for what only you could do and DID for me! I would have happily paid any price for what you gave me! I URGE YOU ALL to schedule a session with this beloved one!

P.S. thank you Barry for sharing her with us all!

*   *   *

Natasha:

I would like to thank Barry for introducing us to Raisa. I have had 2 consultations with her in the last month and I am in total awe of what transpired. Raisa is such a beautiful caring soul! She connected with me as though she has known me forever. Her love and dedication in assisting others is so touching. I had an amazing experience and some profound healing. I received a message from Jeshua which brought tears to my eyes. I could feel the LOVE in the message that was given to me and I will remember and cherish His message forever. Raisa has really helped me in confronting fears, trauma and past life karma. I have found the reason for my skin problems which I never would have thought it'd be possible. It is amazing what guilt and shame from past lives can actually do to your body. Her healing and that from our Angelic beings has really made a huge difference in my life. I can feel it in my energy. Raisa has a lovely sense of humour, always reMinding you not to take life and yourself so seriously. I really feel like a heavy weight has been lifted off my soul. Thank you so much! Much Love!

* * *

Ariel:
Raisa... Divine Raisa... You are a Treasure to this Life, and I thank All That Is, and this also Treasured YT channel for the priceless blessing which was our session this AM. Every moment of the session was a fractal explosion of wonderful intuitive & Divinely guided perfection. I honor your sincere, caring, graceful, playful, soothing, encouraging, transformational, empowering, and so beautiful demonstration / embodiment of Goddess energy and presence. I am so honored & thankful to have been guided to You. To have invested in the patience, time, energy, and resources to share sacred healing and uplifting time with You. I will remember the session Always. And I will look forward to any and all ways our Creator deems it harmonious to connect again. I could go on and on and on, so please accept my parting acknowledgment of your blessing to this realm, my Heart & Spirt, my Life, and the Lives of all those who may be positively impacted via your assistance. Blessings, and Gratitude, a thousand times over and over again. Namaste... Namaste...

Namaste...

*   *   *

B.G.

I have just finished a healing session with Raisa. The experience was remarkable! I am still buzzing! I heard about her from this channel, so thank you deeply Barry!

Raisa is so lovely to talk to, and intuitively guided, knows how to get to the hidden roots of our issues. She calls upon ascended masters, archangels and such to do deep energetic clearing and healing work. It was like being guided through the deep layers of myself, releasing the things that don't serve me and filling every cell with light. I purged, and I absorbed new energy, and came out feeling uplifted and renewed. Raisa helped me to find things in myself that I had been cut off from, and to heal wounds I had tried to bury. She has also given me helpful ideas to continue to improve things my life.

I am so blessed to have found Raisa, and ever grateful for the healing work she has done. She is as authentic as they come. Truly an earth angel! Thank you, thank you, thank you!

FINI

YouTube Channels of Interest:

Giving Voice to the Wisdom of the Ages
Over 5,000 audios, hundreds of
Spiritual and Metaphysical
audio books including
Robert A Russell, Dr Murdo MacDonald Bayne,
Napoleon Hill, Jeshua, Kryon and many more.

I AM Meditations and Affirmations
Hundreds of "I AM" Meditations,
Daily affirmations and more.

Raisin' Your Isness
Metaphysical Musings, Channelings,
Sound Healing Songs